THE NO NONSENSE KEY

Read *The Wines of America*

- If you thought fine wine had to be imported.
- To find out whether California winemakers are correct when they claim that every year is a vintage year.
- If you thought you had to spend more than $10 to buy a bottle of quality wine.
- If you're confused about why some wineries make more than one type of Cabernet Sauvignon or Chardonnay.

NO NONSENSE WINE GUIDE

THE WINES OF AMERICA

Robert Schoolsky

LONGMEADOW PRESS

To Steven, J. L., Diane, and David
And vintages yet to come

ACKNOWLEDGMENTS

My thanks to Robert Mondavi, who walks in the footsteps of Padre Serra and Ágoston Haraszthy and is the "backbone" of American wine; to Rory Callahan, of the New York office of the Wine Institute, for his assistance; and to the Wine Institute again and H. Shenson Int'l. of San Francisco for the excellent map of California and the New York Wine and Grape Foundation for permission to reproduce the map of New York State.

CONTENTS

INTRODUCTION

Even though early settlers from Europe found wild vines and planted their own grapes, wine consumption on a regular basis, with food, was one European tradition that failed to make the transition from the Old World to the New. However, the United States has been undergoing a wine revolution.

In the early 1960s wine sales figures started to climb. Americans had begun to develop a taste for wine, routinely consuming it with meals as well as using it for entertaining. Today, with changing lifestyles and our interest in gourmet food, our appetite for wine has expanded considerably, often at the expense of heavier, distilled spirits such as rum or Scotch.

Wine has become the "in" thing at cocktail parties, and ordering a glass of wine at a bar or tavern no longer causes raised eyebrows. No self-respecting food magazine or newspaper would dream of running a photograph of a table setting without a bottle of wine. This marks a considerable change from the attitudes of only a generation ago. But despite this change, many of us have failed to discover our native winemaking industry, which has raised the quality of domestic wine to a level equal to Europe's best.

In spite of its newfound popularity, most Americans still feel uncomfortable with wine. We tend to set wine apart as something that must be learned and studied, unlike other foods and beverages that are familiar to us. Those of us who really do not enjoy "studying" anything often tend to throw up our hands and solve the problem by simply avoiding wine completely. Others make it an arduous task by enrolling in wine courses and purchasing weighty reference books.

Although there is nothing wrong with wine courses, most of them serve to extend the mystique that surrounds wine, ignoring the basic fact that the enjoyment of wine can be as uncomplicated as the enjoyment of a well-turned steak or a slice of pizza. No one ever had to teach us how to enjoy these two items. We really don't care about how the steer that produced our steak was fed, about where it was raised, or about the tomato content of the pizza. We are concerned only with how it tastes and whether it satisfies our appetite.

Our approach to wine should be the same, and the aim of this guide is to make it so. Over the years a select group of writers and so-called authorities have managed to mystify the subject of wine, leading the average consumer to believe that one must master the entire vinicultural and viticultural processes to enjoy a bottle of Long Island Chardonnay, California Zinfandel, or Pinot Noir from Washington state.

With wine, we have happily been given a natural food product. There is no reason why we cannot enjoy it without burdening ourselves with myriad rules and regulations, which serve only to obfuscate matters. The simple fact is, wine is a food product. It knows no ethnic or class boundaries and can be enjoyed as readily as beer, milk, or soda.

There is a type of wine to go with almost every food we eat, with the possible exception of some soups and salads. Among the various wines, one can find the ideal beverage for pasta, burgers, and even ham and eggs. Wine's flexibility finds it equally at home at a formal dinner party or at a picnic. The only limitation is your imagination, the only complication the operation of the corkscrew. The timid can even avoid that problem by sticking to some of the quality jug wines from California that come in screw-cap bottles.

This No Nonsense Guide contains basic information in an easily understood format and language, allowing you to feel comfortable ordering wine when dining out, entertaining at home, or making purchases at your local retail store. In addition, we hope it will bring you a new awareness of our great domestic wines and the quality levels America's winemakers have attained.

Important information is highlighted at the beginning of each section, and at a glance you can obtain information on how a wine should be served, vintages, food combinations, aging potential, and approximate retail cost for newly released vintages.

You don't need to know the entire vocabulary of the trade or be conversant with technical knowledge of grape growers and vintners, nor do you have to memorize all the names and characteristic styles of every Napa Valley vintner. The most important function of this guide is to impart enough information about wine and how it is made to enable you to guide yourself to the wines of your preference.

Although there are some good reasons for the rules that have evolved around wine drinking, they are not etched in stone. (We know one eminent food critic who pops ice cubes into her red Burgundy!) We will discuss the "rules" and when and why you can ignore them.

Besides the major wine producing states (California, New York, Washington, and Oregon) a number of emerging regions in other states are producing wines of interest and should be noted. For those who want to learn more about these emerging areas, there are a number of good reference guides on the market. However, if this is the last wine book you ever have to purchase, it will have achieved its purpose. If, on the other hand, it whets your interest enough to cause you to delve further into this fascinating subject, we will consider it equally successful.

1

VITICULTURE AND VINICULTURE

Although we care little about how our clothing is made or how cars are manufactured, wine buffs take a deep interest in how grapes are grown and how wines are made. We have raised winemakers to the status of pro-football stars and in some circles the names of such noted winemakers as Heitz, Mondavi, and Nightingale are household words.

Wine production is exceptional in that each harvest differs slightly from others according to the whims of nature. Since such variations have an effect on quality and the price we must pay, a brief summary of how wine is made helps in the appreciation of why some bottles cost only $5 and others $50.

Grapes are grown in almost every country in the world. Quality wine grapes, however, are cultivated in two thin rings that circle the earth in the northern and southern temperate zones. In the United States the wine-grape-producing area starts at the Canadian border and runs down to Los Angeles in the West and northern Florida in the East.

Three factors go into the making of wine:

- The soil
- The climate
- The man

Although grapes will naturally turn into wine without assistance, man has supplied the knowledge to control what nature has provided by way of soil and climate to produce fine wines.

The vineyard calendar has a rhythm all its own.

The tempo starts in early spring and progresses throughout the year until the fall harvest. Some months the vines require a great deal of attention; at other times the grower must simply wait for the grapes to pass through a growth stage.

The Vineyard Life Cycle

The following techniques may differ slightly from one region to another, but basically a typical grower's year starts in March.

March	When the vines begin to emerge from their winter sleep period, the earth must be plowed to uncover the base of the vines and aerate the soil.
April	New plantings of nursery stock and continued plowing as the sap rises in the established vines. Keep alert for possible frost.
May	The possibility of frost continues. The vines are weeded and cleared of insects.
June	The flowering of the vines. In northern climates hail storms and frost are still possible.
July	Spraying and trimming. More weed removal and soil aeration. Grape berries look like tiny green pellets or peas.
August	Weeding and trimming. Black and red grapes start to lose their green hue and take on coloration.
September	Keep birds and deer away from the vines. In eastern coastal areas keep alert for late hurricanes and fall storms. If the vines have received sufficient sunlight, the harvest of most varietals will start at the end of the month.
October	The harvest. At its completion the vines are fertilized to feed the growth of vine wood to keep it healthy through the winter cold.

November	Trim the longer vines. Plow the soil to cover the base of the vines for winter.
December	Begin to prune the vines to prepare for next year's growth.
January	Pruning continues.
February	Pruning ends.

Winemaking

As previously noted, grapes will naturally turn into wine without any assistance. Winemaking is simply the process of fermentation in which natural yeast spores on the skins turn the sugar in the grape into alcohol, producing wine.

Basic rule: Grapes with higher sugar content will produce wine with higher alcohol content. Another basic rule: If allowed to ferment completely dry, the resulting alcohol percentage will be roughly half of the sugar content at the start of fermentation.

If the fermentation stops or is stopped early, residual sugar will remain, as in dessert wines. The winemaker controls the process and determines the style of wine to be produced. The basic steps are the same for red and white wines, with the exceptions described below.

1. The grapes, either red or white, go into a crusher-stemmer, which breaks the skins and removes the stems and stalks.
2. For white wine, the resulting juice and skins pass into a press, which squeezes the juice out into a fermentation tank. In the case of red wine, the skins remain with the juice to add color during fermentation.
3. The wine ferments. Temperature must be strictly controlled during this period. At some point the winemaker will put the red juice through a press to remove the skins and return the grapes to the tank to complete fermentation.
4. When the desired alcohol content has been reached, the fermented juice will go into barrels to age. The

wine picks up wood tannins and the taste of wood from the barrels, the amount depending on the age of the barrels.

5. During the barrel-aging period the wines will be racked. This is a process of carefully transferring the wine from a full barrel to an empty one, separating it from the solids that have fallen to the bottom.

6. The aging period in wood can be a matter of months or years. Before bottling, the wine is usually filtered. It may be shipped at this point or kept for a year or more at the winery for bottle aging.

A Grape by Any Other Name Makes a Different Type of Wine

Wine can be fermented from any grape or fruit—fermentation is natural in nature. However, great wines can be made only from a selected group of grapes. The best wines in the United States are made from a special European type of grape called *Vitis vinifera*. This type embraces such names as Cabernet Sauvignon, Chardonnay, Riesling, and Pinot Noir.

Growers have discovered after experimentation at the University of California at Davis and Cornell University in New York that certain grapes thrive in certain types of soil and in particular climates. A few varietals can be successfully cultivated in many areas, but the wine made from the grapes will differ considerably from area to area. Chardonnay for instance, has many styles and tastes different and exhibits other differences when grown in Napa or the Central Valley in California and when produced in the Finger Lakes region of New York state or on Long Island.

Quality wines come from vines that have been carefully pruned each year to limit the yield. This ensures that the grapes contain as much sugar and body as possible. If yields are too high and vines are not pruned, the sugar-producing process cannot keep up with the demands of the additional clusters of grapes. In such cases yields may be up but quality will suffer. Each grape variety takes a different period of time to come to full ripeness. Early-ripening grapes are usually high in acidity. Grapes that stay on the vine longer, exposed to additional sunlight, will generally be sweeter and yield wines with high alcohol content.

Good vines with deep roots can often produce commercially viable crops for as long as fifty years, although most are pulled up and replanted long before they reach that age. Under the proper conditions, single vines may produce grapes for more than 100 years. This is an extreme exception, however, and grapes from such vines are rarely used in wine production.

No other country in the world has put as much stress on wine varietals as the United States. This emphasis of public identification of the type of wine in the bottle is now being copied elsewhere. In the United States we cultivate most of the leading European strains and some French-American hybrids. The latter are the result of cross-breeding of French and native American grape types. They are grown in the East, particularly in New York. Only a few seem to have been readily accepted by the public. Seyval Blanc appears to be one of these winners. The best-known varietals include:

Cabernet Sauvignon	A red grape. Produces the most expensive and powerful of all red wines.
Chardonnay	Produces the most expensive and popular white wines, which are full bodied.
Chenin Blanc	A white grape. Usually vinified slightly sweet.
French Colombard	A white blending grape.
Gamay	A red grape, related to the Gamay Beaujolais of France.
Gewürztraminer	A white grape. Makes a spicy wine. A late-harvest version makes a great dessert wine.
Johannisberg Riesling	The official U.S. designation of the German white grape. Very aromatic.

Merlot	A red grape used in blending, particularly with Cabernet Sauvignon as a softener. Now gaining popularity as a single varietal.
Petite Sirah	A red grape. Used in blending.
Pinot Noir	A red grape. Difficult to cultivate and vinify.
Sauvignon Blanc	A white grape. Sometimes called Fumé Blanc. Rapidly gaining popularity. It is vinified completely dry.
Zinfandel	A red grape but often used to make "blush" wines. May be related to a European strain but considered native American.

American wines fall into three broad classifications:

Varietals	The predominant wine in the bottle must be from a single grape type. Only 25 percent can be another wine type used for blending purposes.
Proprietary	A better-class blended wine bearing a unique trade name. Adapted by vintners who do not wish to be held to a varietal label, since grape quality changes from vintage to vintage.
Generics	Blended wines that bear a popular name of a European regional wine but bear no relation to the original. These include Burgundy, Chablis, Chianti, Claret, Rhine, and Sauterne.

2

THE VIKINGS
HAD A WORD FOR IT

The actual landing site of Leif Ericson and his Viking band remains shrouded in the mist of time, but his writings confirm that the portion of North America he discovered teemed with wild grapevines. Similar findings were reported by the colonists in Virginia and the Pilgrims who came ashore at Cape Cod.

Early attempts to make wine from these native-American grapes were not very successful, however. Thomas Jefferson, our first oenophile, imported grape cuttings in an effort to duplicate the great wines of France at his home in Virginia. However, the vines failed to develop in the Tidewater climate and soil.

To trace the beginnings of the U.S. wine industry we must go back to the early sixteenth century and the explorations of the Spanish conquistadores who settled California. Hernando Cortez, conqueror of Mexico, brought vine cuttings with him. Following the tradition of church involvement with vines in Europe, he ordered Jesuit missionaries to plant them on their mission grounds.

The Jesuits, who established missions throughout Mexico and the Baja California region, had already tried with little success to make sacramental wine from the native grapes in Southern California. As an alternative they planted a *vinifera* strain from Europe, known today as the Mission grape. Variations of it are still grown in California, although it is not a commercial staple.

The first significant name in California wine history is Padre Junipero Serra, a Franciscan friar who established the mission of San Diego and later moved north and founded Mission San Juan Capistrano south of Monterey. The original buildings still exist in the city of Carmel. His vine plantings produced their first vintage in 1782. Eventually sixteen of the twenty-one Franciscan missions had vineyards and working wine cellars.

The missions grew enough wine for their own religious requirements and the ruling Spanish dons, but commercial wine production did not get underway for some 100 years. In 1824 an immigrant from Bordeaux, Jean-Louis Vignes, planted a vineyard with European cuttings in California.

Later, attracted by the gold rush, Agoston Haraszthy, a Hungarian nobleman, settled in San Francisco and planted grapevines south of the city. At the same time, a contemporary, General Mariano Vallejo, reestablished the neglected mission vineyards in Sonoma. Haraszthy returned to Europe in 1861. With financing from the government of California he purchased more than 100,000 cuttings of 300 different varietals. Even though many of his experiments failed to take hold, Haraszthy is generally given credit for the start of full-scale commercial winemaking in California.

The era of the "Noble Experiment," Prohibition, from 1920 to 1933, saw the end of winemaking growth in every part of the United States. There was some sacramental wine production in California and New York. However, this miniscule output and the manufacture of grape juice failed to save many wineries from bankruptcy.

In the aftermath of Prohibition the industry drifted somnolently until the wine explosion of the 1960s. Today wine production is underway in thirty-four of the fifty states with emphasis on new activity in the Pacific Northwest, Michigan, Texas, Virginia, and New England and a rebirth of activity in New York, particularly on Long Island and in the mid-Hudson region.

11

3

WINE AND FOOD

Sometimes it seems that Americans "taste" wine, whereas in the rest of the world wine is considered an everyday component of the diet, naturally served with all meals. Someone once said, "A meal without wine is like a day without sunshine." An apt phrase, since wine enhances food. So many different types and styles are available that the most exotic dish can be successfully paired with a glass of *vino*. Fortunately America's vineyards offer a truly amazing range of wines, giving us an advantage over our European friends, who generally drink the wines of their region and limit themselves to one or two different styles.

We have all heard the famous "red with meat, white with fish" rule, but this is not a commandment etched in stone. There is tremendous room for variation and experimentation.

Not that the old rule about color lacks all validity: A delicate brook trout, for instance, would be overwhelmed by a rich, heavy Cabernet Sauvignon or Merlot, and a cut of rich prime rib would devastate a delicate, buttery Chardonnay. On the other hand, there's no reason why a juicy grilled salmon steak in red wine should not be served with the same red wine used in the sauce.

The following chart contains suggestions for the marriage of various foods and wines. However, you should experiment whenever you can and discover your own flavor combinations. Let your taste buds and imagination be your guide.

WINE CLASS— BEST-KNOWN TYPES	WINE-AND-FOOD COMBINATIONS

APPETIZER WINES

Sherry	Before or between meals.
Vermouth	Serve well chilled without
White table wines	food or with nuts, cheeses, hors d'oeuvres.

WHITE DINNER (OR TABLE) WINES

Chablis	With lighter dishes.
Chardonnay	Serve well chilled with
Chenin Blanc	chicken, fish, shellfish, pork,
French Colombard	omelets, any white-fleshed
Gewürztraminer	meat. Also serve as appetizer
Pinot Blanc	wines.
Rhine Wine	
Riesling	
Sauvignon Blanc	
Semillon	
Sylvaner	
White table wines	
White Zinfandel and other "blanc de noirs" and "blush" wines	

RED DINNER (OR TABLE) WINES

Barbera	With hearty dishes.
Burgundy	Serve at cool room tem-
Cabernet Sauvignon	perature with steaks, chops,
Gamay	roasts, game, any red meat,
Grignolino	cheese dishes, pasta.
Merlot	
Petite Sirah	
Pinot Noir	
Red table wines	
Rosé	
Zinfandel	

WINE CLASS— BEST-KNOWN TYPES	WINE-AND-FOOD COMBINATIONS

DESSERT WINES

Muscat	At dessert.
Late-harvest types	Serve chilled or at cool room
Port	temperature with fruits, cook-
Cream (sweet) sherry	ies, cheese, nuts, cakes, tarts.

SPARKLING WINES

Champagne	With all foods.
Pink Champagne	Serve well chilled with any
Sparkling Burgundy	food—appetizers, main
	courses, or desserts. Espe-
	cially good in festive party
	punches

Source: *The Pleasures of Wine and Food*; The Winegrowers of California, The California Wine Institute, San Francisco, CA 94108.

Cheese and wine are such ideal soulmates that they deserve special consideration. The best combinations follow:

CHEESE	WINES
Cheddar	California Burgundy
Colby	Gamay
Gouda	Zinfandel
Muenster	Merlot
Tilister	Chardonnay
Edam	Johannisberg Riesling
Monterey Jack	
Swiss	French Colombard
Gruyère	California Chablis Rosé
American Blue	Barbera
Gorgonzola	Petite Sirah
Brick	Pinot Noir
Stilton	
Feta	Grey Riesling

CHEESE	WINES
Mozzarella	Sauvignon Blanc
Teleme	Fumé Blanc
Farmers	Semillon
String	Gewürztraminer
Asadero	
Ranchero	
Gourmandise	
Brie	Cabernet Sauvignon
Camembert	Pinot Blanc
	Schloss

Source: *The Pleasures of Wine and Food:* The Winegrowers of California, The California Wine Institute, San Francisco, CA 94108.

Experimenting with various food-and-wine combinations can be fun. Some wines are very versatile depending on their age and vinification method. One of the most adaptable to any type of food is Zinfandel, a popular native-American varietal. Like Al Capp's famous Lil Abner cartoon character the shmoo, which could turn itself into any food your tastebuds desired, Zinfandel has the ability to be all things to all people. Drink it young, and it's Gamay. Let it hang around awhile, and enjoy Pinot Noir. Really put some age on it, for a mature wine in the Cabernet Sauvignon tradition, tannin and all. Now they're even making white and "blush" wines out of it. Best of all, one need not hock the family jewels to enjoy it. Quality Zinfandel can be as inexpensive as $3 or $4 a bottle. Big spenders can go for broke at $9 and really impress the neighbors.

In its various guises, Zinfandel is a perfect wine to serve throughout a dinner party. Start off with a chilled white version as an aperitif. Uncork a slightly cooled young bottle of red for the appetizer and switch to something in the mature, aged category for the main course. Later, with the coffee, pour a vintage Zinfandel Port type. Keep the labels wrapped and at the end of the meal unwrap the bottles to astound your guests— or keep them guessing and tell them you have a shmoo in your wine cellar.

LAKE & MENDOCINO

SONOMA
NAPA VALLEY

SACRAMENTO

SIERRA FOOTHILLS

SAN FRANCISCO

CENTRAL VALLEY

CENTRAL COAST

SOUTH COAST

LOS ANGELES

CALIFORNIA

4

THE WINES OF CALIFORNIA

From the end of Prohibition in 1933 to 1965, only two new wineries opened in California. From 1966 to 1985, more than 550 licenses were issued. If one individual is responsible for the change in California's wine image from screw-cap jugs to world-class wines, that man is Robert Mondavi. Breaking away from his family-held operation at the Krug Ranch, Mondavi created his own state-of-the-art winery in Oakville.

Even though a few wineries had been making quality wine for decades, they were either unknown or ignored by sneering Francophiles. Mondavi changed our perception of California and its potential. Official figures show that in 1965, the year before Mondavi's solo entry into the business, California had 110,000 acres planted in wine grapes. By 1983 this figure had soared to 363,700 acres.

By the end of the 1960s, "boutique" wineries were springing up all over the state, and the fervor was catching on in other parts of the country. In California, from the Sierra foothills to Los Angeles, entrepreneurs set up presses and French-oak barrels. Doctors, lawyers, engineers, airline captains, and tax-shelter seekers, they were riding the wave of America's wine explosion.

California vineyards produce all the popular grape varietals, and each growing region has developed its own style. Some areas are better than others, and this is reflected in the prices of their wines. Research at the University of California at Davis has developed new strains of grapes permitting planting in regions heretofore considered unsuitable for grape cultivation. It should be noted that there is considerable difference between a Chardonnay made in Napa and one vinified from grapes cultivated in the Central Valley.

Over the years, U.C. Davis has identified five climate regions in California, classifying them according to degree days, the same standard used by weather forecasters to determine the total heat of each season. It's also used by fuel suppliers and homeowners to calculate the cost of heating our homes. The cooler wine regions stretch along the coastal areas, and the warmer regions are in the Central Valley districts.

Region I is quite similar to the European regions of Champagne and the Rhine in Germany. It is best suited for Chardonnay, Cabernet Sauvignon, Sauvignon Blanc, and Pinot Noir. Region II's European counterpart would be Bordeaux and can successfully grow the same varietals as cultivated in Region I. Region III is like southern France and the Rhône Valley, best suited for Sauvignon Blanc, Semillon, and Ruby Cabernet. Regions IV and V are like Spain and North Africa.

Special recognition should be given to the work at U.C. Davis. Not only has the institution played an important part in California's development, but much of its research has been copied throughout the wine world. Its graduates have filled important posts at many of our leading wineries, and its reputation has drawn students from France, Italy, and Germany.

Approved Viticultural Areas (AVAs)

In 1983 the Bureau of Alcohol, Tobacco, and Firearms (BATF) set up the AVA system, which officially recognized individual winegrowing areas in the United States. Though roughly inspired by the European appellation-control laws, our regulations pertain only to geographic regions and bear no relation to wine styles, viticultural procedures, or methods of vinification, as do the laws in Europe.

As mentioned, California vineyards produce all of the popular grape varietals and each growing region has developed its own style. In addition, there are AVAs

18

in every state, and dozens more are in the process of being approved. They can be confusing to the consumer, particularly in the case of California wines, whose labels often bear the name of one AVA, designating the growing area, and also indicate the official address of the winery, which can be in another officially recognized growing area.

For further information on this subject write to the U.S. Treasury Department, Bureau of Alcohol, Tobacco, and Firearms, Washington, D.C., for their publication, *What You Should Know about Grape Wine Labeling.*

California—the Golden Wine State

Unlike viticulture in Europe, where broad regions produce only one varietal, California's growing regions have dozens of unique microclimates. These are small areas with special temperature and geographic conditions. Thus, a grower who owns land in a valley and the side of an adjacent mountain may be able to grow many different grape types on his property.

This chapter will cover the important regions, their microclimates, and their wines in detail.

California Wine Regions

There are five major wine-producing regions in the state, each divided into smaller growing regions, or AVAs. The best-known quality labels come from the North Coast, which contains the valleys of Napa and Sonoma. In addition to the North Coast, this No-Nonsense Guide will cover the regions of the Central Coast, the Central Valley, and the Sierra Foothills.

The last region, the South Coast, which includes the counties of San Diego, Riverside, Orange, Los Angeles, San Bernardino, and Ventura, does not produce wines of wide distribution or of equal quality when compared to the rest of the state and is omitted in this guide. Information on the wines of the South Coast can be obtained from reference books that cover California in greater detail.

California Vintages

Contrary to the old chauvinistic boast, every year in California is not a vintage year. Excessive rains, storms at harvest time, extreme drought in other years, and differences between one microclimate and another can cause considerable differences in the state's wines from one year to another and from one region to another. On balance, however, the state consistently produces wine of good to excellent quality to a higher degree than other states or countries. On all overall basis the following are the best quality vintages for California: 1985, 1984, 1981, 1980, 1977, 1976, 1974.

THE NORTH COAST

Just north of San Francisco, its climate strongly affected by the bay and the Pacific Ocean, lies the North Coast, which contains Napa, Sonoma, Mendocino, and Lake counties. The latter two represent a small part of the overall region, so our emphasis will be on the first two. The North Coast is California's richest growing region and contains many of the state's most famous wine producers.

North Coast/Napa

Famed in song and story, the reputation of Napa Valley wine is on a par with that of the Médoc in Bordeaux. Half the vines planted here are Cabernet Sauvignon and Chardonnay.

The valley starts just above Calistoga in the north and extends in an elongated arc to Carneros in the south. The Mayacamas Mountains, the natural divider separating Napa from Sonoma, form the western boundary. On the east there are a series of minor peaks along the historic Silverado Trail. Carneros, in the south, is partially in Napa, with its western half in Sonoma. It swings around the base of the Mayacamas Mountains, forming a U base for the two valleys.

Napa Valley contains three distinctive temperature zones: The warmest climate is in the north, the central portion is moderate, and the coolest zone is in the south, closest to the cooling effects of San Francisco and San Pablo bays. Wineries and vineyards are situated throughout the valley and in isolated mountain alcoves.

Recommended Napa Wineries and Their Wines

The following Napa wineries are recommended because of their consistent quality from one year to another. The location is the winery's official place of business and not necessarily the location of its vineyards or cellars. Not all the varietal, proprietary, or generic labels produced by each winery are included in this listing. Wines that represent top value considering their retail price in relation to their quality are indicated by a $. A *Q* designation is given to those wines that are outstanding in their varietal or classification regardless of price. The letter *R* after the varietal listing indicates that the recommendation refers to the winery's reserve or special bottling label only.

NAME	LOCATION	BEST WINES	
Acacia Winery	Carneros	Q	Chardonnay
			Pinot Noir
Beaulieu Vineyard	Oakville	Q	Cabernet Sauvignon-R
			Chardonnay
Beringer Vineyards	St. Helena	Q$	Cabernet Sauvignon-R
		Q$	Cabernet Sauvignon
		Q$	Chardonnay
		$	Fumé Blanc
Burgess Cellars	St. Helena	Q	Zinfandel
			Chardonnay
			Cabernet Sauvignon
Cakebread Cellars	Rutherford	Q	Chardonnay
Carneros Creek Winery	Napa	Q	Pinot Noir
		Q	Zinfandel

NAME	LOCATION	BEST WINES	
Chateau Montelena Winery	Calistoga	Q	Cabernet Sauvignon
		Q	Chardonnay
Clos du Val	Napa	Q	Merlot
		Q	Zinfandel
			Cabernet Sauvignon
Conn Creek Winery	St. Helena		Cabernet Sauvignon
		$	Zinfandel
			Chardonnay
Domaine Chandon	Yountville	Q	Sparkling wines
Duckhorn Vineyards	St. Helena	Q	Merlot
Frog's Leap Winery	St. Helena		Chardonnay
Grgich Hills Cellar	Rutherford	Q	Chardonnay
			Johannisberg Riesling
		Q	Zinfandel
Heitz Wine Cellars	St. Helena	Q	Cabernet Sauvignon-R
Inglenook Winery	Rutherford		Cabernet Sauvignon
			Chardonnay
		$	Ruby Cabernet
Robert Keenan Winery	St. Helena		Chardonnay
Hanns Kornell Champagne Cellars	St. Helena		Sparkling wines
Louis M. Martini	St. Helena	Q	Cabernet Sauvignon
			Barbera
Mayacamas Vineyards	Napa	Q	Chardonnay
		Q	Cabernet Sauvignon
Robert Mondavi Winery	Oakville	Q	Cabernet Sauvignon-R
			Chardonnay-R
		Q	Fumé Blanc
		Q$	Red table wine
		Q$	White table wine
		Q$	White table wine

NAME	LOCATION	BEST WINES	
Joseph Phelps Vineyards	St. Helena	Q	Cabernet Sauvignon
		Q	Insignia
			Chardonnay
			Fumé Blanc
		Q	Johannisberg Riesling
			Zinfandel
Quail Ridge	Napa		Chardonnay
St. Clement Vineyards	St. Helena	Q	Chardonnay
			Cabernet Sauvignon
Schramsberg Vineyards	Calistoga	Q	Sparkling wines
Stag's Leap Winery	Napa	Q	Cabernet Sauvignon
Sterling Vineyards	Calistoga	Q	Cabernet Sauvignon
			Chardonnay
			Merlot
		Q	Sauvignon Blanc
Sutter Home Winery	St. Helena	Q	Zinfandel
Trefethen Vineyards	Napa	Q	Chardonnay

North Coast/Sonoma

The Napa and Sonoma valleys both end in the Caneros region in the south. The Mayacamas ridge marks Sonoma's eastern border with the Sonoma chain of mountains separating it from the Pacific in the west. At its northern end are the wine districts of Mendocino and Lake counties.

Sonoma's southern vineyards are cooled by San Francisco Bay. The northern area, with a number of individuals AVA's, is affected by the flow of the Russian River which cuts through the Sonoma Mountains to the ocean beyond. The valley still maintains the feel of old California, particularly the city of Sonoma, where the ancient mission still stands. Visitors can still see Haraszthy's original Buena Vista cellars.

The Russian River area, an AVA in its own right, contains a number of other areas that have gained considerable reputations for quality in recent years. These include the Alexander Valley, Dry Creek, and Knights Valley. In total, Sonoma has around 30,000 acres of vines under cultivation. All major varietals are grown and prices tend to be slightly lower than those of Napa labels. Some of California's best Chardonnay comes from Sonoma.

Recommended Sonoma Wineries and Their Wines

(See the explanation of wine recommendations under North Coast/Napa.)

NAME	LOCATION	BEST WINES	
Alexander Valley Vineyards	Healdsburg		Chardonnay Johannisberg Riesling
Chateau St. Jean	Kenwood	Q	Chardonnay Fumé Blanc
		Q	Johannisberg Riesling
		Q	White table wine
Clos du Bois	Healdsburg	Q$	Merlot
		Q$	Chardonnay
Dry Creek Vineyard	Healdsburg	Q	Chardonnay Fumé Blanc
		Q	Zinfandel
Gundlach-Bundschu Winery	Vineburg		Cabernet Sauvignon Chardonnay
Hacienda Wine Cellars	Sonoma	Q	Gewürztraminer
Hanzell Vineyards	Sonoma	Q	Chardonnay Pinot Noir
Jordan Vineyard and Winery	Healdsburg		Cabernet Sauvignon

NAME	LOCATION	BEST WINES
Kenwood Vineyards	Kenwood	Q$ Zinfandel
Korbel Champagne Cellars	Guerneville	Sparkling wines
Piper Sonoma Cellars	Windsor	Sparkling wines
Sebastiani Vineyards	Sonoma	$ Cabernet Sauvignon Q$ Zinfandel Q$ Jug wines
Simi Winery	Healdsburg	Q$ Cabernet Sauvignon Chardonnay
Sonoma-Cutrer Vineyards	Windsor	Q Chardonnay

THE SIERRA FOOTHILLS

North of the Central Valley, southwest of Sacramento, lie the rugged Sierra foothills and the counties of Amador, El Dorado, and Calaveras. The lesser areas of Modoc, Nevada, and Tuolumne counties are not covered in this book. The important AVAs are El Dorado, Shenandoah Valley, and Fiddletown. In place names that conjure images of the forty-niners and Mark Twain, the earth yields its treasure in the form of Zinfandel, the prevalent varietal in the region.

Little is known about Zinfandel's origin. For years this varietal was used as a blending staple and ignored by most experts. Though it was once one of the most widely planted grape types, its acreage began to fall off in the early 1980s in favor of Cabernet and Chardonnay cultivation. With the introduction of blush wines on a large scale in 1984, vintners discovered that Zinfandel made the best blush because of its intense fruit, and there was a "rediscovery" of the grape. Zinfandel flourishes in the Sierra region, and whatever is not used by wineries within the area is shipped to vintners in other areas.

Recommended Sierra Foothills Wineries and their Wines

(See the explanation of wine recommendations under North Coast/Napa.)

NAME	LOCATION	BEST WINES
Amador Foothill Winery	Plymouth	$ Zinfandel
Boeger Winery	Placerville	Cabernet Sauvignon Zinfandel
Shenandoah Vineyards	Plymouth	Cabernet Sauvignon Zinfandel
Stevenot Winery	Murphys	Zinfandel Chenin Blanc Chardonnay
Stoneridge	Sutter Creek	Zinfandel

THE CENTRAL VALLEY

The Central Valley consists of eight counties: Kern, Tulare, Fresno, Madera, Stanislaus, San Joaquin, Sacramento, and Yolo. A combination of the Sacramento and San Joaquin valleys, this is one of the world's greatest agricultural areas, responsible for 80 percent of California's grape production. More than 200,000 acres are under cultivation for wine varietals, and another 225,000 acres are dedicated to Thompson Seedless. The Thompson was once a widely used blending staple for inexpensive wines. Today it is used primarily in brandy and raisin production and as a table grape.

Most of the wines made in the Central Valley are jug wines, which provide the bulk of all California wine production. Lesser varietals such as Zinfandel, Chenin Blanc, Barbera, and French Colombard are the mainstays. Since jug wines are low priced and depend on large-scale production for profits, one does not find "boutique" wineries in the valley. Instead, there are large-scale operations such as Gallo, Franzia, and

Guild whose labels fill retail shelves throughout the United States.

It is not possible to write about the Central Valley without special mention of the Gallo Winery in Modesto. Not only are they the largest producers of wine in the United States, but their production of some 300 million gallons per year is unequaled by any other winery in the world. The entire operation is still directly controlled by Ernest and Julio Gallo, who share all marketing and vinification responsibilities. Although their reputation is based on nonvintage generic and jug labels, they have started to market with great success a new line of moderate-priced, high-quality varietals.

Recommended Central Valley Wineries and Their Wines

(See the explanation of wine recommendations under North Coast/Napa.)

NAME	LOCATION	BEST WINES
Franzia Winery	Ripon	Chenin Blanc
E. & J. Gallo Winery	Modesto	Q$ Chardonnay
		Q$ Cabernet Sauvignon
		Q$ Zinfandel
		Hearty Burgundy
		Chablis
Papagni Vineyards	Madera	Q$ Alicante Bouschet

THE CENTRAL COAST

This is no doubt California's most diverse and picturesque wine region, with mountain and hillside vineyards bathed in morning fog that protects them from the searing sun. Valley fields are cooled by Monterey and San Francisco bays. The region starts just below San Francisco and ends at the southern end of Monterey County.

The region is sprawling enough to be divided into three subregions, each of which contains a number of AVAs. The Bay Area consists of Alameda, Contra Costa,

San Francisco, San Mateo, and Santa Clara. The North Central contains Monterey, Santa Cruz, and San Benito counties. The South Central San Luis Obispo and Santa Barbara.

For a long time the wines of the central coast, particularly those from the Monterey Valley, were spurned by experts because they carried a flavor and aroma known as the "Monterey veggies." Instead of fruit, wines often reeked of bell pepper and other vegetables. A great deal of experimenting by growers has changed the wines considerably, eliminating the problem by controlling vine spacing and watering methods. Today all the prime varietals are grown throughout the region.

Quality has vastly improved while most prices have remained reasonable, making the wines of the central coast some of the best values on the retail market and on restaurant wine lists. On the other hand, some of the labels from the region have attained recognition for their world-class quality, and their prices are equal to California's best.

Recommended Central Coast Wineries and Their Wines

(See the explanation of wine recommendations under North Coast/Napa.)

NAME	LOCATION	BEST WINES
Almadén Vineyards	San Jose	Charles le Franc varietals
David Bruce Winery	Los Gatos	Q Chardonnay Pinot Noir
J. Carey Cellars	Solvang	Cabernet Sauvignon
Chalone Vineyard	Soledad	Q Chardonnay Q Pinot Blanc Q Pinot Noir
Concannon Vineyard	Livermore	Q$ Petite Sirah Q$ Sauvignon Blanc

28

NAME	LOCATION	BEST WINES	
Congress Springs Vineyards	Saratoga	Q	Zinfandel
Durney Vineyard	Carmel Valley	Q	Cabernet Sauvignon
Edna Valley Vineyards	San Luis Obispo	Q	Chardonnay
Estrella River Winery	Paso Robles		Cabernet Sauvignon
The Firestone Vineyard	Los Olivos	Q	Chardonnay Pinot Noir
HMR	Paso Robles	Q	Chardonnay Pinot Noir
Jekel Vineyard	Greenfield	Q	Chardonnay
Paul Masson Vineyards	Saratoga		Chardonnay
Mirassou Vineyards	San Jose		Sparkling wine Cabernet Sauvignon Zinfandel
Monterey Peninsula Winery	Sand City		Cabernet Sauvignon Zinfandel
The Monterey Vineyard	Gonzales	Q$	Classic Red
Martin Ray	Palo Alto	Q	Chardonnay
Ridge Vineyards	Cupertino	Q Q Q	Zinfandel Petite Sirah Cabernet Sauvignon
Roudon-Smith Vineyards	Santa Cruz		Cabernet Sauvignon
Sanford & Benedict Vineyards	Lompoc		Chardonnay

NAME	LOCATION	BEST WINES
San Martin Winery	San Martin	Fumé Blanc Zinfandel
Santa Ynez Valley Winery	Santa Ynez	Sauvignon Blanc
Ventana Vineyards Winery	Soledad	Chardonnay
Villa Mt. Eden Winery	Oakville	Q Cabernet Sauvignon Chardonnay
Wente Bros.	Livermore	Chardonnay Grey Riesling

5

THE WINES OF NEW YORK

New York wineries have fallen on bad times. While winemakers in other parts of the country have been riding the boom of our new interest in wine, New York, which once ranked second only to California in quantity and quality, has seen grape growers plow up their fields rather than pay taxes on grapes they cannot sell. Some wineries, such as Gold Seal, have closed their doors; others are struggling to stay alive.

The problem with the state's wines seems to be a case of the wrong grapes at the right time coupled with poor geography. The American consumer has displayed a marked preference for dry table wines, particularly white, vinified from the European-style *Vitis vinifera* grapes, which flourish so well in California. New York, because of its cold winters, has always relied on native New York varietals, called *Vitis labrusca*. These grapes make rather sweet wines with a so-called foxy aroma and flavor that does not sell in the current market. Because of the short growing season, New York wines lack sufficient sunlight and are often unbalanced— high in acidity and low in sugar. Sugar is often added to assist in proper fermentation.

In an effort to overcome the problem, the state's winemakers developed a number of hybrid grapes, crossing European varietals with American types. The result is supposed to be cold-resistant vines that bear fruit similar to European stocks. Almost a quarter of the state's production is in hybrids, but with few exceptions such as Seyval Blanc, the resulting wines have failed to find an appreciative market.

Even in sweet kosher-wine production, where the

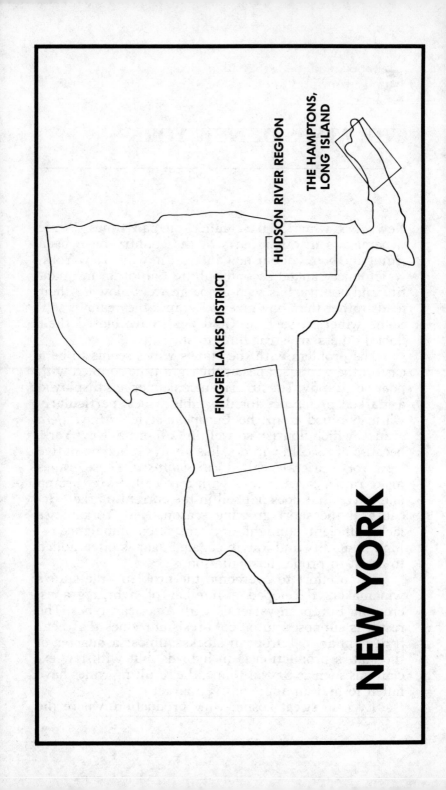

NEW YORK

FINGER LAKES DISTRICT

HUDSON RIVER REGION

THE HAMPTONS, LONG ISLAND

state's wineries traditionally enjoyed a monopoly, sales have been off because of imports of dry type wines from Europe and California. Sale of sparkling wine, another state mainstay, has been surpassed by low-priced Spanish entries and the jump in quality méthode champenoise–type sparklers from California.

The picture is not completely bleak. Two of the state's newer regions are leading a renaissance in winemaking. On Long Island's east end a small band of pioneers have established a number of wineries—"boutique sized" even by California standards—dedicated to European *vinifera*. In addition, the mid-Hudson region, north of New York City and south of Albany, has had success with some of the better hybrids and some *vinifera* plantings.

Upstate, particularly in the Finger Lakes region, a few growers have been able to grow *vinifera*, particularly Chardonnay, in tiny microclimates in which it is necessary to employ special vine cropping and to hold down yields to ensure that surviving stock remains healthy enough to withstand freezing winters. In addition, noting that climate and temperature upstate are similar to those in the grape-growing regions of the Rhine River in Germany, growers are turning to the Riesling with remarkable results in sweet and dry versions.

NEW YORK GRAPE VARIETALS/HYBRIDS

Aurora	A hybrid used in white still and sparkling wines.
Baco Noir	One of the better red hybrids.
Catawba	An old-style foxy eastern grape.
Cayuga	A white hybrid with so-so potential.
Chancellor	A red hybrid related to Rhône wines.
Chelois	One of the few red hybrids to show some promise.
Concord	The basic eastern varietal, foxy and sweet, it is the most widely planted grape in the state.

De Chaunac	French hybrid. Makes a well-balanced red wine in some areas.
Delaware	Old-style eastern white.
Duchess	Old-style eastern white.
Marechal Foch	A better quality red hybrid.
Niagara	Old-style eastern white.
Ravat	A clone of Chardonnay.
Seyval Blanc	A white hybrid that makes a better-than-average table wine.
Vidal Blanc	A white hybrid with potential.
Vignoles	A clone of Chardonnay.

Note: Most of the above grape types are grown elsewhere in the East and the Midwest.

Recommended New York Wineries

The following list highlights recommended wineries that made strides with *vinifera*-type grapes or better-class hybrids. Many of these wines have earned critical acclaim, and their reputations have spread beyond the state's borders. (P) indicates a proprietary blend.

WINERY	RECOMMENDED WINES
Benmarl Wine Co.	Seyval Blanc, Baco Noir, Cuvée du Vigneron (P)
Bridgehampton Winery	Merlot, Sauvignon Blanc
Casa Larga Vineyards	Chardonnay
Finger Lakes Wine Cellars	Johannisberg Riesling, Seyval Blanc
Glenora Wine Cellars	Chardonnay
Hargrave Vineyard	Cabernet Sauvignon, Chardonnay, Merlot
Heron Hill Vineyards	Chardonnay

WINERY	RECOMMENDED WINES
Hudson Valley Winery	Chelois, Chablis (P), Burgundy (P)
Lenz Vineyards	Merlot, Gewürztraminer
Peconic Bay Vineyards	Chardonnay
Pindar Vineyards	Winter White (P), Chardonnay, Merlot, Johannisberg Riesling, Cabernet Sauvignon
Plane's Cayuga Vineyard	Riesling, Chardonnay
Rolling Vineyards Farm Winery	Seyval Blanc
Vinifera Wine Cellars	Chardonnay, Riesling, Pinot Noir
Wagner Vineyards	Chardonnay, Johannisberg Riesling
Wickham Vineyards	Chardonnay
Widmer's Wine Cellars	Vidal Blanc, Seyval Blanc, Johannisberg Riesling
Hermann J. Wiemer Vineyard	Riesling, Chardonnay
Woodbury Vineyards	Johannisberg Riesling, Chardonnay
Joseph Zakon Winery	New-style kosher wines

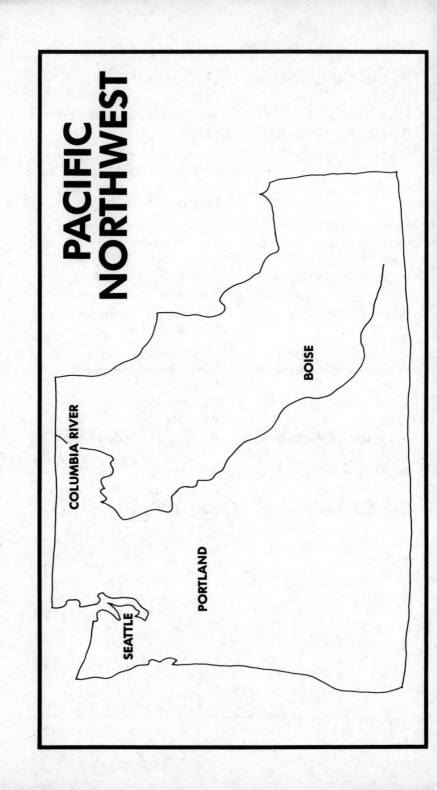

6

THE WINES OF
THE PACIFIC NORTHWEST

The fastest-growing wine region in the United States is the Pacific Northwest, in the states of Oregon and Washington. The latter in particular has shown remarkable growth—from a handful of wineries only a decade ago to more than fifty today.

Most of the wine activity in Washington is in vineyards planted in the vast area called the Columbia River basin, east of the Cascade Mountain range. The area is basically desertlike and arid, but irrigation has transformed it into a very fertile region. With the mountain range keeping away the huge amount of rain that falls to the west, the Yakima Valley is proving an ideal climate for *vinifera*.

With vineyards in Yakima and wineries 150 miles away in Seattle, harvested grapes have had to make the long trek across the Cascades during the night, when temperatures are cool. This will come to an end soon as wineries establish facilities at the vineyard sites.

Winemaking in Oregon, almost all in the Willamette Valley, is much older than that in Washington. There are more established wineries in Oregon but less vineyard acreage. Much of the wine made in Oregon is made from grapes imported from Washington; enlightened label legislation requires Oregon producers to give the origin of the grapes of all wine made in the state.

Oregon law also prohibits the use of generic terms such as *chablis* and *burgundy*. Oregon varietal wines must contain at least 90 percent of the grape type if its name is on the label. The one exception is Cabernet Sauvignon, which must make up at least 75 percent of the contents if so labeled.

The biggest operation in the entire region is Washington's Chateau Ste. Michelle, which now sells around 500,000 cases of wine yearly and has become a major factor on the U.S. wine scene. Owned by U.S. Tobacco, the company boasts Andre Tchelistcheff, dean of American winemakers, as its chief adviser. He has held the post since the winery started operations.

SIGNIFICANT NORTHWEST WINERIES AND THEIR WINES

Winery	Wines
Adelsheim Winery	Chardonnay, Riesling, Sauvignon Blanc
Associated Vintners	Gewürztraminer, Semillon, Chardonnay
Chateau Ste. Michelle	Cabernet Sauvignon, Merlot, Chardonnay, Sauvignon Blanc
Elk Cove Vineyards	Riesling, Chardonnay, Pinot Noir
Eyrie Vineyards	Pinot Noir, Chardonnay
Knudsen-Erath Winery	Pinot Noir, Chardonnay
Oak Knoll Winery	Chardonnay, Pinot Noir
Preston Wine Cellars	Cabernet Sauvignon, Chardonnay, Merlot
Sokol Blosser Winery	Pinot Noir, Merlot
Tualatin Vineyards	Pinot Noir

7

OTHER U.S. WINE REGIONS

As commercial winemaking springs up in various regions around the country, in many states it hearkens back to a tradition of wine growing that dates from our earliest days, with the arrival of the first settlers in Massachusetts and Virginia colonies.

Today there are meaningful numbers of wineries in Idaho, southern New England, Virginia, Maryland, New Jersey, Missouri, Michigan, Arizona, and Texas. Some are reviving wineries closed since Prohibition, and others are entering the field for the first time. With the exception of Ste. Chapelle Winery in Caldwell, Idaho, these wines are rarely seen outside their local regions. Their production is extremely limited, and most of their sales are conducted at the winery or in nearby restaurants and wine shops.

The history of winemaking in the United States is covered elsewhere in this guide, but it is interesting to note here that commercial winemaking originated in the East. The first winery of note was in Cincinnati, Ohio. One Nicholas Longworth produced sparkling Catawba in that city and was doing very well until the Civil War and personal illness forced his operation to close.

8

WINE TASTING

Compared to the rest of the wine world, American consumers are extremely fortunate. Our stores and restaurants carry many foreign and domestic labels, so we often have a wide array of brands from which to choose. Most Europeans drink local country wines throughout their lives, rarely sampling anything that was not grown and vinified in local co-ops.

Since purchasing new wines as they arrive on the market can become rather expensive, tasting wine in formal or social gatherings has become rather popular. Arranging a tasting among a group of friends need not be complicated. This chapter will describe how to arrange a tasting, how professionals sample and rate wines, and the proper wine glass to use to display wine to its best advantage.

Professional Wine Tasting

The expert taster who can slip a glass and recite the country, region, vintage, vineyard, row and vine number, and name of the vintner is a fictional character. Most professionals can tell the grape varietal and usually the general origin of the wine. But with the exception of favorite vintner styles that have left deep impressions over the years, exact origins and vineyards are impossible to determine.

There is no secret to wine tasting. It is a matter of palate memory and record keeping, especially if one intends to be serious about the subject. We can all remember a particular food dish, say apple pie, that stands out in our memory. Every apple pie we have eaten since has been mentally compared to that pie. A professional pie taster, however, would make notes on all the other pies sampled through the years, probably listing the date, restaurant or location of the tasting, type of pie, apple varietal, crust texture, sweetness, and his opinion. Wine tasting is no different.

Record Keeping

The type of records one maintains depends on how thorough you want to be, how many wines you taste during a month, and how you want to store and retrieve your notes. For most, a small pad will do to jot down items of interest about a wine enjoyed in a restaurant or in the home of a friend. This would make an ideal shopping list for your next trip to your local retailer.

Wine tasting on a larger scale requires more detailed notes, which can be filed away for future reference. Index cards are ideal for this purpose, since they are easy to carry and do not require transcribing for filing. Owners of home computers should investigate some of the software packages available that provide more sophisticated record keeping.

You will want to record five basic types of information. They include:

- Wine-identification details
  Country or origin (state, district, etc.)
  Official governmental designation (AOC, DOC, etc.)
  Wine type (varietal, generic, or proprietary)
  Vintage (or nonvintage)
  Chateau or vineyard name
  Shipper
  Date tasted
  Site of tasting
  Price
- Appearance
- Aroma and bouquet
- Palate taste
- Aftertaste

A typical tasting card would look something like this:

Name of Wine: _____ Vintage: _____
(Varietal, Generic, etc.)
Chateau/Vineyard Name: _____ Price: _____
Origin/Appellation _____ Date: _____
Site/Location of Tasting _____

Appearance: Score: _____
Clarity _____
Color _____
Viscosity/Density _____
Comments _____

Aroma and Bouquet: Score: _____
Fruit _____
Others _____
Comments _____

Palate: Score: _____
Sweetness _____
Tannin/Wood _____
Body _____ Acidity _____
Balance _____ Length _____
Comments _____

Aftertaste and Finish: Score: _____
Body _____
Sweetness _____
Balance _____
Lingering Taste _____
Comments _____

Summary   Gross Score: _____
                                               Average: _____
Comments _____

The identification data are self-explanatory and can be obtained from the wine label.

Appearance

This is the first thing one notices about a wine. Clarity and color are important. Hold the glass up to the light or against a white background. Is the wine clear or cloudy? If red, is it light in color, scarlet, ruby, plum, or some shade in between? If white, is it almost clear liquid, pale yellow, straw, or gold? The color of wine is the most important factor in determining how it has aged. White wines tend to get brown around the edge as they mature and oxidize. Red wines start to turn a brick-brown hue, then become dark brown with age.

Aroma and Bouquet

Commonly called the nose. Swirl the liquid in the glass and take a deep sniff of it. Does it smell clean or is it musty or does it carry the aroma of cork? Can you smell the fruit? Try to describe the aroma in simple terms. A chemical analysis is not necessary. One often doubts the tasting notes of many experts who can discern ten different aromas in a particular wine!

Palate Taste

Take a sip, taking some air in the mouth at the same time. Slosh the wine throughout the mouth, over the tongue and palate. This allows you to get all the sensations of sweet and sour in the various taste buds in the mouth. Describe the sensations. Is the wine dry? Is it sweet? Can you taste the fruit?

Aftertaste

Either spit out the wine in a suitable container provided or swallow it. If the original taste was fruity and pleasing, how is the aftertaste? Is the taste lingering or sharp and biting? If a sweet wine, is it oily and clinging or fresh? How is the fruit in relation to the acid, both of which comprise the body or structure of the wine?

Scoring and Rating

A number of complicated professional scoring systems are used in the wine industry. For most consumers the basic questions are, was the wine enjoyable and would one want to purchase a bottle? This can be noted by a simple overall judgment in a few words or a scoring system that rates the wines on a scale of 1 to 10.

Outstanding wines would receive the highest score. Usually anything below a 4 or 5 should be avoided in the future. Remember, taste is a highly objective sensation that can vary considerably from one person to another. The purpose of a tasting record is to make your own determination, not to keep track of the opinions of others.

Planning a Tasting

Tastings usually have a theme, such as all reds or whites selling within a particular price range. Other themes might compare new issues of a particular varietal, wines by region, varietals from one country to another, etc. Vertical tastings usually involve wines from a single chateau or producer, covering a number of vintages. A horizontal tasting includes wines from a number of producers, all of the same vintage.

Logistics

Most tastings are held "blind." In other words, the bottles are covered with paper and taped so participants know nothing about the wine. In this case each bottle should be numbered. A place mat with circle outlines containing glass numbers is ideal for keeping track of wines in a blind tasting. The tasting location should be well lit. A white tablecloth or a white background is preferred. Scoring sheets and pencils should be provided, along with "spit buckets" for those who wish to use them.

Someone should be delegated to pull the corks on all bottles so as not to delay the actual tasting procedure. If aeration is needed, decant the wines beforehand. If not, the corks should be reinserted in the necks of the bottles by hand so they can easily be removed later. White wines should be prechilled. Room temperature should be cool.

Slices of French or Italian bread, breadsticks, or plain crackers should be on hand. After each wine is tasted, a morsel of bread or a bit of cracker will clean the palate, so that new flavors can register clearly. Cheese should not be served in a formal tasting session. It tends to overpower the palate. French wine négociants have an old saying, "Buy on bread but sell on cheese."

The most important tool is the tasting glass provided. An ideal glass is reproduced below.

Source: Club de Gourmet Editorial Group, Club G.S.A., Velayos 4 (bajo), 28035 Madrid, Spain.

A good tasting glass need not be expensive. It should be completely clean and not carry any soap residue or film. The glass should be clear without color and free from any etching or design. The glass and stem should be thin.

45

9

STORING AND SERVING WINE

Until recently storing U.S. wines for aging purposes was not a big problem. The general opinion among experts was that our domestic wines did not last long and had no aging potential. This was partially due to the sales policies of the wineries, since they rarely held back any stocks but sold all of each vintage as it was bottled. Few maintained a "wine library" that would furnish any historical record to track the evolution of their wines.

Another factor was the myth voiced by many in California that "Every year is a vintage year." Cheerfully fostered by the chamber of commerce and the wine industry, the slogan implied that each year's wine was the same, so aging was not necessary. The situation changed when the "wine explosion" of the 1960s brought "new blood" to the industry. Outsiders opened wineries at a hectic pace, and research strides were made at the University of California at Davis concerning differences in microclimates and vintages. Wineries began to keep stocks of wine under proper cellar conditions, to form a basis for comparison in future years.

Today there is no question that our red wines improve with age in the manner of great European wines. The only question is, how long will they last? Time alone will furnish the answer. A few years ago I had the opportunity to taste a number of BV vintages going back to 1945 and 1940, with remarkable results. The wines, particularly the 1940, were superb. Unfortunately, with central heating, air conditioning, and lack of space, our homes and apartments are poor places for long-term wine storage.

Expensive Alternatives

A well-known wine collector in New York has solved the problem of storing wines by maintaining his home at a constant 55 degrees all year-round. "I carefully explained to my fiancée before we married," he relates, "love me, love my wine collection." The system works for him, although it is rather amusing to see their maid cleaning the apartment in an Eskimo parka. Another collector, a noted physician, purchased the apartment on the floor below his Park Avenue residence to store his vintage collection.

The Real World

Few of us can afford this luxury. For us, the difficulty in keeping wine over a long period remains a thorny obstacle. In an era of immediate consumption, when many consumers have neither the money nor the space to create a wine cellar, many winemakers are accommodating them by fermenting wines that are ready to drink when released by the winery.

Site Selection

For those who do want lay down wine for aging, three factors should be kept in mind when planning a proper storage space. Although wine is not as fragile as some experts would have us believe, its great enemies are:

- Light
- Noise and vibration
- Temperature variations

Ultraviolet rays in many light sources can prematurely age wines. That is why quality reds, meant for aging, come in densely tinted bottles.

Noise and vibration usually go hand in hand. If

wine is stored in a high-traffic area where children run or play or near a machine that goes on and off, the wine will be affected.

The rise and fall of temperature in the average home is ruinous for wine. Even if you live in a private residence, your basement is not necessarily the ideal "cellar," any more than is the hall closet in an apartment adjoining the central hot-water pipes.

Closets that are constantly being opened and closed are poor wine-storage sites. Contrary to interior decorators and Hollywood set designers, the kitchen with its activity and heat generation, should be avoided. On the other hand, although 55 to 60 degrees is ideal, somewhat higher temperatures are acceptable if they are *constant*. At worst higher constant temperatures will cause wines to mature faster.

Do It Yourself

If you're handy with tools, a closet can be quickly and inexpensively converted into a cellar by lining the walls and door with insulation. A hole cut into the door or wall can house a compressor unit for cooling. The entire job should run about $500. A larger space can be created by dividing a room or walling in an area in the basement. Basement locations should be away from fuel burners and areas reserved for entertainment.

Commercial and Prefabricated Units

Self-contained storage units range in size from walk-in models capable of housing hundreds of cases to small models that can serve as end tables. They can be purchased by mail order or through local distributors. The larger units usually have dual temperature chambers for red and white wines, and some feature humidity controls. Prices start at around $500.

Off-Premises Storage

There are a few alternatives to a custom-built cellar. Some public warehouse firms maintain proper facilities for long-term storage, but this can be expensive and access can be difficult. In addition to storage fees, in-and-out charges must usually be paid each time you add or remove a case. If you're a good customer, your local wine merchant may permit you to store your case purchases in his cellar. But beware—his cellar conditions may be worse than yours!

Serving Wine—Temperatures

Americans have a frosted-palate syndrome, cultivated by ice-cold milk, frosty colas, and frozen shakes. This is reflected in our wine preferences. We are decidedly devoted to white wine, perhaps because whites can be chilled, whereas reds are forever cursed with the ancient dictum "Serve at room temperature."

When that rule for wine serving was etched in stone, "room temperature" was 65 degrees year-round, so reds were actually served quite cool. To duplicate those pre-central-heating conditions, even the finest red wines are enhanced by a brief twenty- to thirty-minute rest in the refrigerator just before serving.

Certain reds can be served chilled—certainly not at the same temperature as a six-pack of beer, but at reasonable settings that enhance their flavor and improve the "quaffability factor." Very young reds, fermented to be consumed at an early age, are at their best when served cool. Lower temperature hides some of these wines' brashness. Gamay (an American version of Beaujolais), Zinfandel, and certain Pinot Noirs fall into this category.

Care must be taken not to overchill. The ideal is 55 to 60 degrees. A few degrees' difference can hide the wine's fruit and a great deal of its body. Chilling serves to decrease some of the volatile constituents in the bouquet and on the palate. Some foods that are ideal with chilled young reds include:

- Chinese Food
- Any other Oriental cuisine
- Frankfurters

- Hamburgers
- Pizza

Whites and rosés should not be overchilled; 50 degrees is a sufficient level for serving without killing the delicate texture of white wine. Most restaurants keep their bestselling whites on ice so that they are at the proper temperature when brought to the table. If a white is too cold, cup the glass in your hand to warm it slightly. You'll appreciate the difference.

Breathing

At this time, few American wines have reached the stage where breathing is necessary. Very young wines and older vintages often require a breathing period to allow the wine's aroma to develop. Contrary to popular belief, a bottle of wine does not breathe if you simply pull the cork. Only the small surface area of the wine in the neck will receive any air if you use this method. The simplest procedure is to pour the wine into a carafe or decanter if breathing is necessary.

Decanting

Most wines, reds in particular, throw off a sediment as they age. Sediment is a natural part of the wine's evolution and does not indicate that the wine is bad. The sediment is not harmful but should be removed, since we want to drink our wines, not chew them.

In decanting, care should be taken not to shake the bottle, since this only distributes the sediment. Carefully pull the cork and slowly pour the wine into a decanter without setting the bottle down until finished. Watch the wine through the neck of the bottle. As soon as sediment appears, stop pouring. A candle or other light source behind the neck will help to spot the sediment, particularly when the bottle is tinted green.

Wine Baskets or Cradles

The original purpose of wine baskets and cradles was to ensure that an old bottle remained horizontal during the trip from the wine cellar to the table. The sediment was not disturbed in this position, and the cradle assisted in the decanting procedure. Once this wine was decanted, the basket served no other purpose. The use of such a device today is an affectation and somewhat dangerous, since it is clumsy.

Order of Pour

Just as menus start out with light foods, building up to a heavy main course, wine selection for dining should follow a similar pattern. Generally speaking, white wines should be poured before reds, and younger vintages should precede older wines. During a typical formal dinner party, featuring three or more courses, wine should be served as follows:

Hors d'oeuvres	A light aperitif wine or Champagne
Appetizer	The same aperitif wine or a Sauvignon Blanc
Soup or salads	Wine is rarely served with either dish
Fish course	A full-bodied, mature white such as Chardonnay
Main course (meat)	A medium-aged Pinot Noir
Cheese Course	A well-aged Cabernet Sauvignon
Dessert	Champagne or a special dessert wine

Ordering Requirements

Wine consumption can vary considerably. Today's lifestyle has cut down on the use of distilled spirits for predinner drinks, substituting wine. A formal, sit-down dinner party, such as the one described in the above chart, is a lengthy affair. A relatively large amount of wine will be consumed, since it is being absorbed with food. Such a menu would require at least one 750-milliliter bottle of each wine type for every two or three diners.

Glasses

For very formal dinner parties some hosts prefer to have a separate, special glass for each wine course. This is not necessary. A single standard-purpose glass, such as the one pictured in chapter 8, Wine Tasting, will suffice. However, for those who wish to follow traditional wine-serving practices, the following glass types are suggested. All should be thin stemmed, clear, and free of any decorations or facet cuts. They should be clean, dry, and free of any aromas or soap film.

Red wines   A glass that holds about 5 ounces of wine. Slightly tulip shaped but not as elongated as the Champagne glass described below. The top rim should be narrower than the bulb-like bottom, to hold in the aroma.

White wines   Smaller than the red-wine glass, it should be slightly wider at the rim to allow for breathing.

Champagne   An elongated tulip-shaped glass is best. Avoid the flat sherbet-type glasses often used at weddings and in restaurants. They are not proper and are used by commercial establishments only because they are easier to store and transport.

10

PURCHASING WINE

The average consumer faces a series of hurdles in the marketplace when he or she embarks on an excursion to the local retail shop to purchase wine. The majority of the clerks one finds at the retail level simply do not have any knowledge of or experience with wine and are in no position to give advice or make recommendations. The problem is one of education. Wine distribution does not differ from the traditional marketing of distilled spirits, so on the wholesale level one finds order takers who may be familiar with Scotch and rye but know nothing about Cabernet, or Chardonnay.

The same problem exists at most restaurants. Training programs are very rare, so waiters and managers can rarely give a diner any advice on suitable wines to go with menu selections. It is an unfortunate situation, since statistics prove that shops and restaurants with well-prepared wine-sales programs and trained staffs sell more wine and earn higher profits.

As a reader of this book, you have more information than the average waiter or clerk and should be able to wend your way through restaurant wine lists and knowledgeably purchase wine at retail.

BUYING WINE AT RETAIL

Since wineries are springing up all over the United States and Americans love to have an excuse for an outing or day trip, a visit to a nearby winery is not only educational but an opportunity to taste a number of wines before making any purchases.

For most of us, the nearest winery is only a few hours' drive away. Your state agriculture department can supply you with a list of wineries and their visiting hours, tour facilities, etc. Almost all of them have some type of retail operation connected with the winery. Prices may not be any lower than at a retail shop, but you will have your questions answered and an enjoyable experience at the same time. Case discounts are almost always given, and an added side benefit is the knowledge that the wine has been stored under the best conditions.

In this country we have never been completely able to shake off the stigma attached to the purchase of wines and spirits. Many of the complex laws governing the sale of alcohol still carry certain elements inherited from Prohibition. Supervision of these laws is up to the individual states, so the pricing of wine and the places where it can legally be purchased can differ according to your place of residence. Some localities have state-run stores. In other areas, wine can be purchased at supermarkets and even drugstores. A recent new development is wine auctions, which have been introduced in Washington, D.C., and Illinois.

The following recommendations refer to most states that license individual package stores selling spirits and wines. The majority of these outlets are "mom and pop" operations that exist on sales of popular distilled spirits for the last-minute Saturday-night shopper who runs out of vodka or Scotch just as the party is in full swing.

Their stocks of wine are usually skimpy and limited to well-advertised jug wines. The single benefit to be found in such shops is that almost all of them keep some white wines under refrigeration and can supply a chilled Champagne on a moment's notice. However, don't look for a great Napa Cabernet or Chardonnay hidden among the bottles of Thunderbird.

No matter where you live, your local newspaper has a day of the week when it publishes a food section. On this day one can find the heaviest concentration of alcoholic-beverage advertising, which provides the best way to determine which retailers offer the widest range of labels and brands. Such stores usually have the best prices because of volume and turnover. Their staffs should be knowledgeable and happy to answer your questions and give advice.

The following section outlines some of the items one should bear in mind when shopping at retail and the services one should expect from a well-run wine shop.

Markups

The average bottle of wine can pass through as many as six levels of markup before it arrives on your dealer's shelf. Suggested retail price can often be a third above wholesale, and many states have set minimum retail markups.

Discounts

Dealers with large inventories often give case discounts and work on a few dollars' profit to keep up their volume. It pays to shop around. Some thought should be given to forming a buying group with a number of friends to give all of you greater purchasing power and bargaining leverage.

House Brands and Direct Purchasing

Many large retailers buy direct from wineries in California and other states. Their bulk purchasing eliminates a number of middlemen, resulting in lower prices to the consumer. Such wine sometimes bears a "house" or private label and can often cost 50 percent less than comparable brands.

Inside Information

If you buy a great deal of wine, it would pay you to subscribe to your local wholesale buyer's guide, which lists the wholesale and suggested retail prices of all wines and spirits offered for sale in your area. With this information, you have an edge when shopping, since you know how much the retailer pays and whether the distributor is offering specials on case lots. One-year subscriptions cost around $35.

Odd-Lot Bargains

Many retailers regularly wind up with a few loose bottles after selling many cases of wine. These wines, as well as wines that may be starting to grow too old for sale, are often grouped together for an "end of bin" promotion. Check them carefully. A forgotten nugget or two can often be found in such a group.

Buying Schedule

Plan your purchases to take advantage of yearly specials and sales. Champagne and sparkling wines are least expensive before Christmas and New Year's and in June for the wedding season. Wine shops do the bulk of their sales shortly before Christmas, and prices are at their best at that time.

Someone has to pay for the cost of aging quality wine. If your dealer does the job, he will increase the cost of his inventory each year as his investment goes up. If you have the proper "cellar" conditions, buy wine as it is released and age it yourself.

Availability

If your retailer does not stock a specific wine that's listed in the local wholesale guide, he should be happy to order it for you. Such orders do not have to be in case lots, since distributors will gladly ship single bottles. This is particularly true with older vintages. If your retailer won't provide this service, change shops.

Tastings

Many shops run tasting sessions on or off premises. Others sponsor wine clubs. At either of these, new releases are sampled, and often visiting winemakers discuss their offerings. Retailers are invited to regular trade tastings; if you are a good customer, ask whether you can go along to sample wines before committing yourself to case purchases.

Winery Visits

If you are planning a trip to the wine country, your dealer can arrange for "insider" visits to many smaller wineries normally closed to the public. Such assistance does require some work on the part of the retailer, so he will be more obliging for regular clients who buy in volume.

Storing Wine

Many retailers are equipped to store case purchases for clients for specific periods. There may be a charge for this service. Check the physical site before entering into such an arrangement, since the retailer's "cellar" may be less ideal than your hall closet.

Information and Advice

The staff of a well-run wine outlet should have up-to-the-minute information on new releases and vintages. They should have in-house tastings on a regular basis. Good clients are often invited to attend these sessions. If a clerk has been particularly helpful, consider giving him or her a gratuity. This will establish you as a serious buyer and will reflect in the attention and service you receive in the future.

ORDERING WINE IN RESTAURANTS

It's difficult to calculate how much wine I've ordered in restaurants over the past thirty years, but it's safe to say I've watched the corks pulled from around 4,000 bottles in hundreds of places around the world, ranging in class from glittering haute-cuisine palaces to the local pasta parlor—slightly more than a couple of bottles a week.

The amazing statistic is that over the years I've had to turn back only two bottles of wine. This does not mean that the other 3,998 bottles were perfect. Only a few dozen were truly memorable. The bulk proved to be drinkable, and a fair portion were on the borderline. I've encountered far more bad bottles of wine at home and during formal tasting sessions than in restaurants.

One goes to a restaurant for the food. Wine is also a food product. Management should give as much consideration to the wine list as to menu planning. For most establishments, wine is an afterthought. A restaurant with a good cellar and a fine list is not difficult to spot. The moment you walk in the door and look around you can tell the quality of the wine list: If the majority of the tables have wine bottles on them, the house has a good list.

Restaurant Pricing

All restaurants purchase their wine at wholesale. They pay the same price as your local retailer. The markup differs considerably, however. This is understandable, since a restaurant has additional costs and overhead such as serving and breakage. A fairly priced list will be marked up not more than one and a half times retail.

Wine by the Glass

Some establishments have an active wine bar and sell a wide range of wines by the glass. These are dispensed by a machine called a Cruvinet, which uses nitrogen to keep uncorked wines from spoiling. This new trend provides the consumer with a good opportunity to sample different wines. Most restaurants, however, stock a house wine that they offer by the glass. Don't hesitate to ask the name of the wine, and if you wish, ask to see the bottle. But remember, house wines are often barely potable, and drinking wine by the glass is the most expensive way to order wine.

If four people are dining together and all want either red or white wine, purchase a full bottle. Consider a half bottle for two people if available. The savings are considerable.

Wine Lists

Most wine lists are prepared by local distributors who print them for restaurants on a complimentary basis in return for getting the bulk of the establishments' wine and spirits order. These lists are usually thick leatherette albums, adorned with labels, lacking any vintage or shipper information. These may look impressive, but they don't give you much help in choosing a wine.

A well-prepared wine list should give the name of the wine, its type, the country and region of origin, shipper or producer name, and vintage. At least 90 percent of the items listed should currently be in stock, and management should not substitute a vintage or winery without permission. Differences in such situations should be pointed out immediately and not left to the diner to discover.

Wine Selection and Ordering

Wine and food complement each other. Thus your choice of wine should be made with reference to your choice of food. Before going through the list ask the waiter or captain what wine he would recommend to go with your food selection. His advice need not be followed. Some California wines are extraordinary in that they go well with a wide range of food. A Zinfandel can be the perfect solution if one of your party chooses chicken and another veal or a light meat dish. But also ask if there are any wines of interest on hand not included on the list. The odd bottle, left over from previous lists because of insufficient quantity for inclusion in a new printing, are often bargain priced.

Some lists bear the warning that older vintages are ordered at the customer's risk. Old American wines are rare and very expensive. Discuss them carefully with the waiter or captain. Unless you are prepared to accept a wine that may have started to oxidize and you have a palate that can appreciate it and weigh it, avoid them. Older wines require a great deal of experience to understand their nuances, and at the prices that many restaurants charge, experimentation can be quite costly. As a general rule avoid old white wines unless you know the cellar very well.

The best buys can be found in the mid-price range. These wines, reasonably priced, are not too young (a problem on most lists) and not too old. Turnover is brisk, a reasonable assurance that you will receive a bottle in good condition.

If the list has a bin number or bottle number, be sure to use it when giving your order. This will eliminate any confusion between you and the captain. If vintage and other information is missing, ask about them. It may be time consuming, but it may prevent misunderstandings later on. If in doubt, ask to inspect the bottle.

Presentation of Your Order

When a bottle is brought to the table, make sure that you check the label carefully before the cork is pulled. The three V's—vintage, vineyard, and varietal—should match the information on the list. Some restaurants will switch wines when they run out of one type. Refusal should be made before the bottle is opened. Never accept a bottle that is brought to the table uncorked unless you're ordering house wine by the carafe. Bottles should be brought to your table unopened. The uncorking ceremony should be performed in your presence after you have inspected the label. Refuse any bottle that does not exactly match your order. If you decide to accept a lesser wine, make sure of its price.

Tasting and Accepting Your Order

When the cork is presented the only thing you're called upon to do is to check the name of the winery burned into the cork, to make sure that it agrees with the label. Don't bother to sniff the cork. Most times it will have the smell of cork, which is natural and does not necessarily mean the wine is "corky."

Squeeze the bottom end of the cork. It should be stained with wine. It should also be moist. Both are good indications that the bottle was properly stored on its side. If the cork is dry and crumbly, air may have entered the bottle, causing the wine to oxidize (see chapter 8, Wine Tasting).

(Incidentally, contrary to popular opinion, few faulty wines actually turn to vinegar. This occurs only under certain bacterial situations that permit the development of a vinegar "mother." A bottle that actually becomes vinegar is a rare find. It should be saved and stored in a cool place, and you should add leftover wine from time to time, drawing off true wine vinegar as needed.)

A small sample of wine should be poured into the host's glass for sampling and approval. If it's a white wine, check the temperature of the bottle. If it has been prechilled, sometimes over-iced, the wine should not be placed in an ice-bucket. Tell the waiter to leave it on the table. He may think this odd, but be persistent. Wine glasses that have been pre-iced should be replaced with clean, dry glasses. Wine is not a martini.

Few U.S. wines require breathing unless they are very young or very old. The latter is a rarity in most restaurants. A red wine may have some sediment and may therefore require decanting. This is the usual procedure for old vintages. Sediment formations are natural and not necessarily indicative of a flaw in wine.

Rejection of a bottle of wine in a restaurant should be a simple, straightforward matter. Management is expected to be gracious, accepting the bottle without question under the assumption the diner has good grounds for refusing acceptance. Finally, be firm. Serving bad wine is as unforgivable as serving bad food. Either should be refused if it fails to live up to its promise. If enough patrons stood their ground, a lot of restaurants would learn the "rules of the game."

11

MYTHS ABOUT WINE

There are many myths and rules connected with wine. Some of them are valid. Most are fiction, based on ancient conditions and wine lore no longer applicable to today's lifestyle. Unfortunately, a great deal of nonsense has attained the status of holy writ, managing to confuse and frighten those whose simple aim is to enjoy a good bottle of wine with dinner. Some myths and breakable rules include the following:

Letting the wine breathe

The moment of decision comes when the waiter brings your selection to the table and asks, "Shall we let the wine breathe?" Most red wines purchased in the average restaurant and almost all whites have no need to breathe. Older vintages and some young reds can benefit from aeration, which is best attained by decanting and not just by pulling the cork and letting the bottle stand. In the latter case only the tiny circular surface area in the neck is exposed to air. Aeration can also be achieved by simply swirling the wine in a glass.

Cork sniffing

I once saw a diner chew on a cork presented by a waiter. Some people react to a cork as if they have been offered a new form of nasal spray. Neither is necessary. The cork should be checked to see whether the name branded on it agrees with the label and whether the "business end" is moist. A dry, crumbling cork indicates that the wine may have been stored upright, allowing air to enter the bottle and cause oxidation.

Ice baths for white wines

Alexis Lichine, the noted wine writer and chateau owner, once observed, "Americans are born with refrigerators in their mouths." Just as food loses flavor if it is too cold, nothing more completely destroys the flavor of a good bottle of white wine than overchill. Fifty degrees is the proper serving temperature for most whites. If the bottle has been stored in a cooler or refrigerator for an hour, plunging it into an ice bucket is destructive.

White wine has fewer calories

This is akin to the belief that a slice of bread is less fattening if it has been toasted. All things being equal, a glass of white wine has as many calories as a glass of red if the alcohol content and residual sugar are the same. Most regular table wine registers 12 percent alcohol and is vinified completely dry. As a matter of fact, low-alcohol white wines, such as German whites, often contain more calories than red varietals.

Champagne lasts forever

Everyone seems to have a bottle or two of Champagne left over from a wedding or other memorable celebration. These bottles are kept and treasured for decades, often stored in the guest closet or in the bottom bureau drawer. Most of the mail that crosses a wine writer's desk asks about the longevity of the wine and when it should be opened. Champagne will last a little longer than other white wines, becauser of its carbonation and acidity. But it will not keep for decades and should be consumed as soon as possible, since it is ready to drink when released by the producer. Vintage Champagnes should be consumed within eight years of the date on the label if properly maintained. Otherwise, find someone who is launching a ship.

Serve red wines at room temperature

When this one was etched in stone no one had ever heard of central heating. The veteran actor C. Aubrey Smith was often posed standing before a roaring drawing room in those old Alexander Korda films of the 1930s. His backside was warm but the glass of Claret in his hand was at 60 degrees; "room temperature." Store reds at 50 degrees and bring them to the table just before serving. Higher temperatures emphasize alcohol at the expense of bouquet. This emphasis, due to heat, is the reason many people complain that a glass of red wine makes them sleepy.

White wine with fish, red with meat

This is the most widely followed adage concerning wine. It is basically correct but is too often slavishly followed. The ideal is to match food characteristics with the proper wine. Since most fish is light and delicate, it goes best with a light wine. But since there are light reds available, white need not be the only choice. When in doubt, drink what you enjoy most, remembering, "A meal without wine is like a day without sunshine."

12

GLOSSARY

Many of the words and terms used in the world of wine in the United States are based on European phrases and traditions. A complete glossary would fill a volume larger than this book. The following listing consists of words one is most likely to come across on wine labels and wine lists. They will be very helpful in understanding the language of the vine.

Acerbic: A coarse, hard taste that comes from unripe grapes.

Acid: All wines contain some acidity, but wine is deemed acid if the acidity level is out of balance with other elements, such as fruit and tannin.

Aftertaste: The effect and taste left behind after swallowing. See *Finish*.

Alcohol: The percentage of alcohol in a finished wine after fermentation. Normal table wines range between 10 and 14 percent alcohol. BATF regulations permit wines to vary up to 1.5 percent from the alcohol level stated on the label. Usually wines with less than 10 percent alcohol are sold as low-alcohol, or "light," wines. To determine the proof, simple double the alcohol percentage; for example, a wine with 12 percent alcohol would be 24 proof.

Alcoholic: Used to describe a wine when the alcohol is noticeable. This can be discerned either in the bouquet, in the mouth, or during the aftertaste.

AOC: From the French Appellation system of place names. The BATF recently instituted a geographical place-name system in the United States. See *AVA*.

Appellation: The designated origin of the wine. Controlled by law. (See *AOC*, above.)

Aromatic: Wines that have a very intense aroma, either

from the grape or developed by the winemaking process.

Astringent: A wine heavy in tannin, which causes a puckering of the lips and has a dry effect on the palate.

AVA: Approved Viticultural Area. A specific geographical winegrowing region that has been given appellation status by the BATF.

Backbone: An expression coined by California winemakers to describe wines with strength and substance, able to go with heavy and rich food.

Balanced: An ideal wine with all the elements (fruit, alcohol, and tannin) in perfect harmony.

BATF: Bureau of Alcohol, Tobacco, and Firearms. A branch of the U.S. Treasury with the responsibility of supervising the wine industry.

Big: Describes an intensely flavored wine or one with a high alcohol content, yet in balance.

Body: A combination of the wine's strength and aroma.

Bottle sickness: An unsettled stage just after the bottling, before the wine has had a chance to adjust to its new conditions.

Bouquet: Those sensations discerned by the nose. The elements of bouquet are developed during fermentation.

Breathing: Aerating very young or old wines to allow the aroma to develop properly.

Brick: A shade of red-brown used to describe certain wines.

Brut: Very dry, as in Champagne.

Cooked: Made from grapes that have been exposed to heat. See *Oxidized.*

Corky: Used to describe a wine that has taken on the smell and taste of the cork.

Crystals: Tiny clear crystals usually found in white wines or on the cork. Do not indicate any problem with the wine; they can be ignored.

Cuvée: A batch, barrel, or cask of wine.

Delicate: Used generally to describe white wines that are light in style but well balanced.

Dry: A wine without any residual sugar after fermentation.

Earthy: A unique aroma reflecting the smell and characteristics of the soil where the grapes were grown.

Estate bottled: A term defined by U.S. regulations as a wine grown in vineyards owned by the winemaker and bottled by the maker.

Fermentation: The process by which grapes become wine.

Finish: The tastes and sensations after swallowing.

Forward: Used to describe a wine that exhibits maturity and complexity at a young age.

Foxy: Used to describe the aroma and taste often found in some native North American grape varietals.

Flabby: Used to describe a wine lacking the proper amount of acidity.

Fruity: Having the taste and aroma of the natural grape. Not to be confused with sweet.

Honest: Used to describe a simple, well-made wine.

Lees: The deposit found at the bottoms of wine barrels.

Legs: the viscous ribbons the wine leaves on the side of the glass after swirling. Not especially significant but nice to look at.

Maceration: The technique of extracting color from the grape skins by leaving them in the juice.

Maderized: Describes wine that have become oxidized and have taken on the taste of Madeira to a considerable extent.

Méthode champenoise: The process used in making genuine Champagne.

Must: The stage of juice after pressing or crushing but before fermentation is complete.

Négociant: A broker or middleman.

Noble: Used to describe a wine with elegance and structure or one of the great grape varietals.

Nose: The combined effect of aroma and bouquet.

Oxidized: The wine has been exposed to air and has started to go bad, usually due to a bad cork or poor bottling procedures at the winery.

Petillant: A slight bubbly aspect to certain young wines. Often detected as a slight prickling sensation. Will often disappear after wine has had a chance to breathe.

Racking: Draining wine from one barrel to another, leaving behind the lees, or dregs.

Robe: The color and visual aspect of the wine in the glass.

Sommelier: A wine steward in a restaurant.

Tannins: Acids in wine deriving from the pits and skins and from oak aging barrels. A red wine needs sufficient tannin to age properly.

Tête de cuvée: Top of the cask; the best wine.

Thin: Used to describe a wine without sufficient acidity and flavor.

Varietal: A specific type of grape, such as Chardonnay or Cabernet Sauvignon.

Viniculture: The science of winemaking.

Viticulture: The science of grape growing.

Volatile acidity: A fault in winemaking detected in the aroma and taste. Causes a prickling sensation on the palate.

Woody: The taste of wines that have been wood aged too long.

ABOUT THE AUTHOR

Bob Schoolsky calls himself a "wino who got lucky." Since his first visit to France at the age of sixteen, his interest in wine and fine food has developed over the years leading to a regular column, "On Wine," for New York's *Newsday* and an expanding waistline.

In addition to his column, he frequently contributes feature stories on food, wine and travel to the paper's weekly food and Sunday magazine sections. His work has appeared in the *Wine Spectator*, and *Grappa*. For two years he served as eastern editor for *Wine and Spirit Buying Guide* and was North American editor for *Vinetec Presse*, a French trade publication, for three years. He is currently writing a guide book on Long Island Wineries.

Not limited to print media, Bob did a daily five minute radio show, "The Audio Vine" during morning drive time on station WVNJ-AM. He is often called upon to do guest appearances and tastings before all types of groups and teaches and lectures on a regular basis before the Wine Club at the International Wine Center in New York and Kevin Zraly's Wine School at Windows on the World.

Bob is a member of the Commanderie du Bontemps du Medoc et des Graves and a member of Compagnon de Beaujolais. His wine writing is geared to the average consumer with emphasis on everyday drinking wines with food. Readers comment on the fact that his columns reflect his own enjoyment in an easy to follow, often humorous style.